Writing Your Own Book

How to write and publish your own book in a flash

Table of Contents

So You Want to Write a Book?

One of the best things that you can do to help grow your business and to position yourself as an expert in whatever field you may work in is to write your own book.

The problem is writing a book can be hard even if you are a seasoned writer.

In this guide were going to talk about different ways that you can have your own book completed by this time next month regardless of if you decide to write yourself or if you choose to take the easy route and have somebody else write it for you.

I would not have believed it if I hadn't done it for myself. You can actually write a book without actually doing the writing. Because of an interesting legal twist, you can hire a writer, and then when the writer is finished, you own the complete copyright to the work. If it sounds too good to be true, it almost is!

What's Your Book about?

It couldn't be easier to select a topic for a book. People are hungry for information, and people are looking to the Internet to feed their hunger. After you've read this chapter, you will feel confident enough to choose your own topic, or you can literally pull your book topic directly from this book and use it! How's that for a deal?

Finding That Aha Moment?

If you're smart enough to read this book, you're smart enough to look around you and determine what interests you and those around you. Think of what problems you've recently solved, and what kinds of problems others have had and solved. Any problem that has been solved in your world could easily be the subject of your next book. People love to read how other have solved a problem that they currently have.

So, **brainstorm** a list of problems in your life and in the lives of those around you. Your friend Bob lost his job? Your sister's child had chicken pox? How did they cope or find solutions? While you're at it, start another list of unsolved problems evident in your corner of the world. Write down problems you wish you had solved. Aha! These are subjects that people will really be interested in! How to lose the last ten pounds. The truth about UFOs. The straightest path to becoming a millionaire. From your personal corner, your step-granddaughter is pregnant at age 14? Your grocery bill is double what it used to be? Your roof leaks? These are problems waiting for solutions!

These unsolved problems would also be great book topics. Remember, you don't have to know the solution, just the topic. You're going to get someone else to do the research and write the book for you. You will not actually be writing one word.

Can You Say Google?

The Internet is a great way to find out what people are looking for at any given moment. You can search for almost anything. Google™ is a popular search engine you can use, or you can try any of the others like Yahoo!. Type in phrases like "top concerns of Americans," "best-selling nonfiction topics," or "popular how-to manuals."

And While You're on the Internet...

Find out the most popular nonfiction books from the New York Times bestseller list, Amazon, and a Google search for best-selling books. Your findings will tell you exactly what book subjects people are buying right now.

Try this. Go to www.amazon.com. From the tabbed menu running along the top of the Amazon home page, click "Top Sellers."

I did this one day in September 2011 and found a Harry Potter book, several other fiction books, and titles such as Natural cures "they" won't tell you about, How what you wear can change your life, How to profit from the demise of the dollar, and The official SAT study guide. I've paraphrased to some degree, but you get the idea.

Here's what I learned just from spending a few minutes on Amazon that day. People are reading good fiction from already-best selling authors (Da Vinci Code, the Harry Potter series, the Girl with the Dragon Tattoo and others). Secondly, Amazon buyers, buying over the Internet, are interested in nonfiction topics such as improving their lives and making more money. For these books, just about any author will do, even virtual unknowns or people who went to prison for lying to the American public.

And that quick visit only confirmed that **the straightest route to book profits is in the nonfiction book market.** This is for a number of reasons. Fiction readers tend to like to curl up in a chair with an actual book. Some of them attend book clubs where the physical books are brought around someone's kitchen table with wine and cheese. Fiction readers tend to purchase from authors they're already familiar with. Fiction can be more difficult to write and deliver well. Also, many of the classics in fiction are available as free ebooks. A reader interested in fiction could just download those. So stick with nonfiction unless you're feeling particularly bold and experimental.

Here is some more good news, and if you didn't already know this then you are going to be smiling big. Drum roll please... **ideas are not copyrighted**, therefore any idea you see, hear, or read anywhere anytime, is yours to use for a book! You can create books around the same ideas that are covered in the Amazon best seller list, and turnaround and create a book on the exact same subject!

Now, copyright law does protect the **way** ideas are expressed, so you want to make sure your hired author does not plagiarize or copy book text outright. And you cannot use the title word for word either. But there's nothing stopping you from creating another book or ebook that covers the same subject with a different voice. It's all as completely legal and guilt-free as nonfat Haagen Dazs. This is why looking at bestseller lists is a great way to get topic ideas.

Digging for Gold

There are groups of people who are willing to buy nonfiction books: **hobbyists**. At any given time, these people are looking for ways to spend their money on their hobbies. Their passion is your financial gain.

What avid hobbyists want will always make great book material. Note that I did not say what hobbyists need. You may have certain opinions on what exactly certain people should need or should read. But those are not necessarily good topics for immediate book publishing profit. Those topics may be areas for you to dabble in at your leisure. However, if you want to make money at this, find out what niche groups want, and hit those groups with your book.

Find hobbyists and niche groups by searching the web for "popular hobbies," "enthusiasts," or "what America is buying." Or, you can search specifically for forums and discussion groups for hobbyists. In the forums, people talk with each other to share ideas with one another. Often, they will exchange testimonials for equipment, upcoming events, and books.

One popular site where hobbyists go to talk to one another online is Yahoo!. Check it out. Go to www.yahoo.com. Click "groups." On the groups page you'll see a list of categories such as Business & finance, and Religion. For demonstration purposes, click on "Games."

On the games screen, game subcategories are listed followed by numbers. The numbers indicate how many discussion forums are available for that subcategory. These numbers reveal a lot. Notice how "role playing games," and "video & computer games" have factors of ten or in some cases factors of 100 more forums than other subcategories. "Wargaming" and "paintball" don't even come close, although those categories are much more discussion-laden than "horseshoe pitching."

For fun, one day I continued selecting subcategories until I arrived at a list of over a thousand (yes a thousand) discussion groups on Yahoo having to do with vampire role playing. Here's how I got there: Games>>Role Playing Games>>Live Action>> World of Darkness>>Vampire: The Masquerade.

Some of the forums are open to new members, and you can join to read what everyone's discussing. Once in the forum, you can review discussion threads from today, yesterday, or a year ago. Don't go back too far if you want to find out the hottest possible book topics. You can participate in discussions if you like. FYI, do not drop into a discussion group just to market a book; hobbyists consider this spam and will drop you from the group.

When you read and/or participate, you'll find out what this group is buying. All you have to do is skim to find out what questions they are asking each other about products or traveling or information. What they are interested in buying is a key piece of information because passionate consumers love to research before they buy. This is an immediate book market. Create a book on how to select the best this or that on the market, related to the current wants of the enthusiasts.

Enthusiasts come in all shapes and sizes. Think brides-to-be, golfers, whitewater rafters, people who collect vintage baseball cards, wine connoisseurs, gardeners, frequent vacationers, video gamers, and parents who put their children into private tutoring, ballet, and violin lessons before age 3.

There are some hobbies that seem to continually attract enthusiasts, like playing golf, watching football, restoring old cars, and listening to music. These are classics. Then there are some hobbies that seem to come and go in waves, such as Red Hat Societies participation, snow boarding, or line dancing. Pick either a classic hobby or a fluctuating hobby in its peak season for your best odds.

A big market on the Internet is the 20-30 set. Here's what they are doing right now, according to one survey. They're snowboarding, wakeboarding, traveling, camping, listening to music, taking photographs. They're drinking gourmet coffee, rock climbing, playing guitar, camping, dancing, looking for online love, shopping for computers and other electronics, attending sports events, studying the Bible, exercising, trying to find jobs, and watching movies. Any one of these subjects would make a great book with a buying market standing by.

Online Training

There is almost no limit whatsoever on the marketability of how-to books. Everyone wants an instruction manual, advice, and encouragement that they can do anything they read a how-to book for. Anything you know how to do, anything you've ever wanted to learn, or anything that's teachable at all, can become a how-to book.

How-to books for hobbyists are a good way to go, and this overlaps with the discussion above. A hobby how-to book could be anything from how to build a home from hay bales to how to play Texas Hold 'Em to how to understand Shakespeare.

One book publisher knows how hungry we are for how-to information, and has created a whole series of "Dummies" books around the market. Further, there are other similar book series', and all of them are doing quite well! "The Everything" series, "Idiot's Guide" series and others are all cashing in on the how-to phenomenon.

You could cash in by creating books on any or all subjects covered in any of those series'. Go to www.dummies.com, and check out their list of titles. Pick one you like, and move full speed ahead!

Remember that even though the books have "Dummies" in the title, that the books are as popular as they are because the readers are not treated like dummies at all. The authors cater to a person who wants to find out the easiest way to do something without too much tangential discussion. When you have your book written and when you choose a title, make sure you are appealing to a reader's smarts! If you use words like stupid, dumb, or hopeless in the title, make sure that it is clear that the meaning would not extend to insulting the individual reader.

Ebooks, because of their brevity and because they are marketed primarily on the Internet can target smaller audiences. You don't have to write a universal book like How to use a computer (which may not be interesting enough to sell anyway in this decade). Ebooks can cover more specific territory. Knowing this, you can 1) create your book in a specific way for a specific niche readership, and 2) create additional books for different facets of the same subject, and sell each one separately!

Say you've decided to write a book on fishing. (FYI, this is one of those hobbies where enthusiasts are willing to spend money!). You could create "How to Catch Freshwater Trout," "How to Tie Your Own Flies," or "How to Plan a Successful Deep Sea Fishing Trip." Almost anything related to the hobby can become a separate book depending on how much detail you include. Clearly, "How to put on waders," probably wouldn't be a great choice (though some would say it's impossible to underestimate today's consumer), because you would have to strain to fill up 60 to 100 pages on such a simple topic. You get the idea. The topic would need to be, in most cases, book worthy. Use good judgment.

Then, life itself requires instructions, as we know from "Life's Little Instruction Book." So, life also qualifies as a good how-to book topic. There are numerous subtopics, and you'll never run out of ideas. Here are a few examples:

- "How to ensure your child gets an A+ in math"
- "How to have a successful garage sale"
- "How to organize your home office"

And while we're on the subject of how-to books, I'd like to make one quick point. The titles of these books do not need to be incredibly clever. Be sure the words "How to" are the first part of the title, and the rest should tell exactly what the book is about.

For example, which of these three titles would be best?

1. "How to have a successful garage sale."
2. "One weekend away from a cleaner house"
3. "How to sell your old shoes for a profit"

Although numbers 2 and 3 are clever, a little punchy, and correspond with the book content, I would still recommend using title number 1. "How to have a successful garage sale" sums it up pretty well and will catch the eye of an Internet surfer who is interested in putting together a garage sale and needs a how-to manual.

Anyway, back to the point. Any phase of life, way of coping with life, or large or small thing about life can be the subject of a how-to book.

Looking Young

Perhaps sixteen year old girls don't want to look younger, but from that point on, and for most of the population in Western society, looking young is a common desire. Everybody wants to find the fountain of youth, whether it be in a pill bottle, a special diet, surgery, or a book.

A book about staying or appearing young in the face of growing old will have a solid future. Here are some title ideas, and I'm sure you can come up with a truckload more.

- "Drop ten years and ten pounds in ten days"
- "How to look 28 forever"
- "100 ways to look younger"
- "Grocery store products that will help you look younger"
- "Look 30 again without surgery"
- "How to live to be 100"

This topic is red hot. Botox, surgery, chemical peels, lasers, diets, acupuncture, electronic pulses, mega vitamins, prescription teas, thigh cream, and teeth whiteners are being purchased by baby boomers, the elderly, and even women as young as 20 ! No one wants to look a day older than they have to.

Health

Health is a concern to anyone who is growing old or ill or faced illness with a loved one or wants more energy or, basically, everybody. Health books are a good investment for you to make. And doctors don't have to be the authors. Anyone with any credentials, or no credentials at all, can write books on health. Just be sure you don't claim to be a doctor if you're not one.

Here are some health topics you can hit at this moment in time and be almost guaranteed immediate interest, readership, and sales!

Disease prevention and cure. As our baby boomer population ages, most will be afflicted with heart disease, cancer, diabetes, dementia, or some other malady. Give these people some hope. Create a book on how to cope, how to find the best practitioners, how to avoid disease triggers, or cures American doctors are unaware of.

Natural remedies. People are curious about alternatives to standard medicine, and are anxious to try herbal, natural, or holistic treatments. Create a book on any disease that covers alternative cures. For example, "How to Treat Lymphoma, Naturally." Or, you could just address natural supplements in general, "The best natural remedies for common ailments," or "Holistic health."

Diet. What we eat is always a hot topic. There are literally dozens if not hundreds of diet fads currently out there. Pick any one of them for a book. Then there's obesity, general health, and also diet supplements like vitamins. Think "How to equip your kitchen for macrobiotic dieting." Or, "Eat to cure cancer."

Travel

Never has so much travel been available to so many. People today want to get in touch with the people they love. They want to experience different parts of the world. See exotic things. Be entertained. Also, because, especially in America, adults sometimes work well more than 40 hours a week, people need really good vacations. They're doing their research to make sure that they will really enjoy their precious few weeks off each year.

Here are some topics for you: how to trade frequent flyer miles, how to keep airport security off your back, how to travel on a dime and get change, and how to keep your children happy on long car trips.

Beyond the how-to's, there is plenty of room for books like, the best amusement parks for your money, top 100 campgrounds, things you must see and do in Utah before you die, and free things to do when visiting Washington, D.C.

Get the idea? The good thing about creating travel books is that you may already know a lot about a place that other people may be interested in visiting. Makes it easy!

Money

Money makes the world go around (well that and the earth's axis and planetary forces), and so it would make sense that books would abound on the topic of money. They do, but the market is nowhere near saturated. There's always room for more. From getting rich to just saving money day-to-day, people are always interested in how-to books related to money. Ideas below:

- "How to feed your family on less than $40 a week"

- "How to get free stuff"
- "How to pay almost no taxes"
- "How to buy a retirement home for no money down"
- "How to be richer than your parents"
- "How to buy cars at auction"
- "How to start a financial management business"

Life enrichment

In these days, although fewer and fewer are attending churches, more and more are flocking to purchase self-help books. Self-help books are leaping off shelves at brick and mortar bookstores. People want to feel that if they read a self-help book, they have all the power to change their lives. Whether or not this is true is moot. Changing your life, soul searching, and helping thyself, are all great book topics.

As much as ever before, people want to know how to find peace with their pasts, how to be creative or spiritual in a consuming society, and how to find true love. There is no end to how-to books you could create in the category of self-help, or life enrichment. Here are a few more ideas here:

- How to marry for life
- How to unbreak your heart
- How to stay sane in a crazy world
- How to meditate

A few more topics bound to explode

These are fiery hot topics that are sure to be on the rise. You can pull any one of these to use for your first book. Then come back and pull another topic for your next book.

Using the latest electronics. We are a society obsessed with having the latest and greatest technology. Do a book on iPods, email/camera cell phones, wireless Internet, digital TV, or any combination of these items.

Home improvement. There's so much of a craze in this area that do-it-yourself (DIY) stores are on every corner of major cities. If you haven't been to a Home Depot or Lowe's lately, then you are one of the few. Sure, apartment dwellers and young students aren't in this market, but people with homes and money to afford them are in this market. In fact, some cable TV services offer entire channels dedicated to home improvement.

Especially of current interest are in-home automation systems. DIY home improvers are eager to learn about and buy things that will make their home lives more relaxing, high-tech, or fun. Create a book to teach them how to make their lights come on for them before they get home from their jobs, or how to press a button to adjust window blinds, music, or temperature. Or how Bill Gates' house works. Or how to add automation to an existing home, or how to build-in automation when a house is constructed.

Identity theft prevention. Especially because many books are marketed on the Internet, this is a great topic. This is because people who purchase over the Internet are concerned that their credit card numbers will not be seen by others or misused in any way. Even away from the computer though, consumers are on-edge about identity theft. Today, people are shredding their receipts, removing their personal information from the face of their checks, and cautiously covering themselves when they type in passwords at public terminals or ATMs. Microchips are being installed on ID cards. People are worried. Tap into this with a book!

Safety. Along the same lines as worrying about identity theft, people are worried about their safety from other things like crime, chemical warfare attack, and natural disasters. Watch the evening news tonight, and you will be able to list at least twenty things that people are afraid of. When you talk about safety, you are speaking their language. Titles along the lines of be prepared for any natural disaster would go over well, as would those like never be a crime victim again, how to defend yourself in a parking lot, or prevent sudden infant death syndrome (SIDS).

How-to manuals for any new product recently on the market. This harks back to the Dummies series but takes it one step further. Target your book to people who want to buy the most current commercially available item. How to use the new model John Deere tractor. You will be sure that no one else has a book like yours, and you can say so in your sales pitch.

How to survive any phase of life. People face numerous demons and battles as they live their lives. For many, when they're in need, they'll be reaching out for help. Support groups, private therapy, being with friends, starting over - these are all solid topics for a book. You could also reach out specifically to certain people needing emotional assistance. How to get through the terrible two's. How to cope with a cancer diagnosis. Living with your own shortcomings. How to live with someone who is dying. Surviving high school. Any of these will do.

Anything to do with pets. People are pampering their pets more than ever before. Some pets are treated better than people. It's the people who spend small fortunes on their pets that will also be willing to pay good money for a book that gives them ideas on how to treat their animals even more royally than they already do.

Write books on how to pamper your parakeet, homemade meals for picky dogs, where the pet spas are, how to train your kids to be cat-friendly, million dollar homes for mutts, which animals make the best pets, or pet psychology.

Traveling mixed with the subjects above. Not only are people traveling like crazy, but they want to customize their itineraries and their methods of travel with their hobbies and lifestyles. Try a few of these on for size: where to dine around the globe and still stay on a low-carb diet plan. Hotels with the best exercise facilities. How to travel exquisitely with large dogs. Crime-proof your campsite. Be creative. There's a market here.

Using the Internet to meet people. As I said, the craze is upon us. Everyone's online, and sometimes folks spend more time chatting with Internet buddies than they do talking face to face with actual friends. I know I've been guilty of this one myself. Anyway, along with the advent of the World Wide Web, came people who need a little help figuring out how to get where they want to get. They want to find like-minded people, find a date, find love, find support.

There's a huge book market for hooking people up with people online. Here are just a few things that could be covered: speed dating online, virtual music jams, taking online classes, hooking up with people who share your hobby, and finding online support groups. Any of these and more are of interest to people who wish to get maximum benefit from their ability, thanks to the Internet, to network with people in the farthest reaches of the world. In fact one of the appeals with online communing is that distance does not matter. Help these people in foreign lands find each other with a book.

Topics of special interest to women. The facts don't lie. Women dominate the Internet, and they spend or influence spending of 80 cents for every dollar changing hands. What women want has never been so important to business owners and authors.

Certain topics appeal particularly to the female set. These include beauty, health, decorating, emotional support, and life enrichment. Women do a few things, generally, that men don't. They play bunko, wear make-up, and talk for hours to their girlfriends on the phone. They send more greeting cards, prepare more casseroles, and vacuum more often than men. They eat more salads and go shopping more often for clothes. They get more pedicures and love to dance more than the average man.

There are two things to keep in mind with regards to women and books. If you want to attract a female market, you need to write about a topic that women like to read about, and you want to make the title friendly towards women.

Here's a female-oriented subject and title: Where to find great shopping bargains in Taos. And here's a male subject: Where to catch the most fish in Taos.

Here's a female-friendly title (same as above): Where to find great shopping bargains in Taos. And here's a male-friendly title on the same subject: Keep your money in your pocket in Taos. See the difference? Know your market, and if you need to choose between one or the other, you're safe going with the women's title.

Sex. People don't need to sneak out of bookstores with erotic books in their hands anymore, and they know it. They are looking on the Internet for sex materials, toys, and books. The Internet is private, individuals can take their sweet time, and indeed they can surf with or without a lover sharing their chair. There's been a recent ebook success entitled Orgasms for two. There is room for more similar ebooks. On the subject of sex, this is one case where a fiction book may also do the trick. You could create erotic short stories or a how-to-have-great-sex ebook. Either ebook would entice adults interested in this category (and incidentally, most adults are indeed interested in this category).

Chapter 2

--Where to find great writers--

When you hire for a writer for your book, what you are doing is enlisting the services of a **ghostwriter**. A ghostwriter is a writer who publishes under someone else's name, with the consent of both parties.

Traditionally, ghostwriters have been and are still today hired by celebrities to write autobiographies when the celebrities are not talented writers. Ghostwriters also sometimes create works for well-known authors, such as Tom Clancy. This practice is done for business reasons, because the author's name alone will sell the books, no matter who actually wrote them.

Ghostwriters may also write for book series' that don't actually have a real-person author. An example of a series written this way is the Hardy Boys series you may remember from your youth. The Hardy Boys cover author, Franklin W. Dixon, does not actually exist. Many romance novel series' have also been created in this way, where the author name on the cover represents any number or variety of commissioned writers.

With the advent of the Internet and books, today, ghostwriters also write books. When you outsource your book to a ghostwriter, you are giving them the job of creating the words in your book in exchange for a fee. You still get to put your own author name on the finished product. Ultimately you will own the copyright, and you can sell the book as many times as you like. If it sounds like a pretty nice arrangement, it is. It's all completely legal and commonly done. And you do not have to be a celebrity or Tom Clancy to hire one.

Great things about ghostwriters

Just because a ghostwriter does the writing does not mean that you do not deserve to be the credited author. You will be the originator of the idea, and provide direction to the ghostwriter, so that the written material reflects what you want it to say. You may also create a pen name for yourself if you wish your real name to remain anonymous to casual readers.

Once you hand off the reins to a ghostwriter to prepare a book for you, you may never go back and try to write one yourself ever again. A ghostwriter can do so many things for you, from researching to editing. And any writer knows that the process of writing and polishing a book or a book takes a significant amount of time. Much more than most readers will ever know. Start-to-finish writing is a large task best left to those who love their jobs, who are willing to spend the time writing and re-writing incessantly until things are just right, and who has talent and experience in the craft.

What they can do

You can outsource more than just rote writing to a ghostwriter. In fact, ghostwriters can be hired to research your topic fully on the Internet or elsewhere. They can then translate your or their research into organized sections and create palatable, conversational paragraphs for your readers. They can interview people that you designate or that they seek out for the book.

They can separate the book-worthy material from non-book-worthy material for inclusion with an eye on what readers are interested in and what you have hired them to write about. In other words, good ghostwriters will stay on the topic as they write and not veer off into irrelevant tangents. It's actually an art form in itself to be able to insert quips and images that are designed to hold a reader's interest while quickly and smoothly getting back on track to deliver the information promised by the title and table of contents.

Speaking of the table of contents, an experienced ghostwriter can review rough notes from you and propose a title and table of contents. Ghostwriters can start from notes, organize the material into an outline, generate a table of contents, research and add filling text, make boring information flow like an entertaining conversation, and more. They can basically start with whatever you've got to start with and get you from there to a completed book.

If you have already tried your hand at preparing a book, a ghostwriter can whip your existing draft book into sell-able shape. She can review the content, make suggestions, do necessary research, add new sections, repair grammar, or revise any not-quite-perfect portions of the book. In fact, it has been known to happen sometimes that one ghostwriter will be hired to edit another ghostwriter's work. This may be done in a case where you are not satisfied with the result from the first ghostwriter, or can also be done if you just want to polish your product - going on the two heads are better than one philosophy.

She can use a writing style and language that is appropriate for the book. Should it be in first person like this book is? Or perhaps it would work better in third person like many reference books are written. Should it be written from a female or male perspective? Ghostwriters will accommodate your preferences, and if you don't know your preferences, ghostwriters can help you make those decisions.

She can put the book into the format that you choose. If you want your pages to appear the size of regular notebook paper (about 8 ½ inches by 11 inches), then the writer can prepare the manuscript to fit. If you like large margins, where the text appears in-between in a narrower column, the ghostwriter can do that. Narrow column books are popular, and easy on the eyes. If you like a blank page preceding chapters, ask for that. For items such as page dimensions, font, and layout, she can make recommendations. She can also, in most cases, provide you the electronic file type that you prefer (MS Word, WordPerfect, Adobe Acrobat, Internet html, or other), or make suggestions to you on format.

Finally, good ghostwriters can write quickly. Ghostwriters cannot perform miracles, but it's not unheard of to get a book done in 30 days when you need it fast. Depending on your need and schedule, you can usually find some who will work even more quickly. It's nice to allow six weeks, but not necessary.

You can sit back while your e is being written

All you need to do is give the ghostwriter the information and he can get straight to work. You may provide any level of detail on your title or topic, your notions (if any) on how the topic should be covered, and any other relevant information. Most of the communication can take place by email, and that keeps things pretty simple and also well-documented. You may, if you prefer, talk by phone or use regular mail. It's not common or necessary to meet face to face with your writer to get her rolling on your project. This is because ebooks tend to be on tighter schedules and lower budgets than ghostwritten bookstore books. It will save time, money, and any confusion, if you try to use email and the Internet as your primary tools to communicate with your writer.

Ghostwriters are invaluable resources. Time is money, and you want to spend your time elsewhere (marketing, thinking of new ideas, relaxing at the beach), ghostwriting is definitely the way to go. The general advantages are that outsourcing the actual writing of the book is not too expensive, commonly done (it's legal and writers are available to provide the service), and you can direct your energy somewhere else while the book is being written. In the end you'll still own the written words, and can do whatever you want with them. Indeed you can even edit and revise them yourself! Next, I'll talk about finding those available ebook ghostwriters and touch also on pricing.

Where ghostwriters lurk

You can find ghostwriters the hard way or the easy way. The hard way is to locate writing or authoring organizations in cities around the globe, and interview writers until you find one that you believe is qualified to write your book.

The easy way to find a ghostwriter is to go to an Internet site where ghostwriters are hanging out, ready to respond to classified ads. You place an ad for your project, and you wait for bids to come in. Two large sites with gobs of ghostwriter of traffic are Elance and Guru.

A third way is to contact ghostwriting companies directly.

Of the avenues available, I recommend going through one of the large sites that have high ghostwriter traffic. Sometimes these types of sites are called freelancer databases, ghostwriter banks, freelancer job banks, or similar.

Get ghostwriters competing for your ebook

The two large online freelancer databases where ghostwriters lurk that I mentioned above, Elance and Guru, operate in essentially the same way. Basically, you post an ad and wait for responses. You choose a writer from the list of responders, agree on a schedule and fee, and then move on and do something else until your ebook arrives to you in your email inbox.

Both sites maintain catalogs of people who provide freelance services. The Elance catalog has over 50,000 people listed. Some of the people in the catalog, or bank, provide software programming or other service. Not everyone in the bank is a ghostwriter. So when you get to the site, you'll need to navigate to the area that applies to ebooks and ghostwriting. Although this may take you a few minutes at first, the site is easily navigable once you get your bearings. Let's walk through Elance.

Go to www.elance.com. From the home page, scroll down to the menu along the bottom of the page, and click on "Marketplace." From the marketplace page, look to the left hand side of the screen, and from that menu, click on "Writing & Translation." If the site organization has changed slightly since this writing, just use common sense and navigate around until you find the ebook projects database. Basically, you are looking for the area where you can advertise that you want to outsource a book to a ghostwriter. Click around until you get there. To make things easier on future visits, when you find ebook outsourcing services, add that URL to your Internet browser's favorites list.

> *Tip:* Writers are referred to as "service providers" on Elance. This phrase is not to be confused with an Internet service provider (ISP) or the service of the Elance web site itself. On Guru, writers are referred to as "registered professionals."

In Elance's writing marketplace, browse through others' ads to see how they are finding ghostwriters, and roughly what the projects are paying. With a quick browse you can see how ads are written and which ghostwriters have responded, and additional details about the advertisers and the ghostwriter responder.

Placing ads is free as of this writing. The ghostwriters are the ones who pay to review the ads. Isn't that nice? You will need to "subscribe" however, and get some of your information into the database in order to advertise. This is only fair so that responders know what they are responding to and so that there is trust that payment will be made when the job is completed.

I recommend that you subscribe right away, so that the processing can take place while you're getting your other pre-work done (selecting a topic for your ebook and creating your ad for posting).

Once you place an ad, writers will begin to post online bids for your project. They may offer to write your ebook for less money than the maximum pay you stated in your ad, or they may offer to write the ebook more quickly than you've stated you require. Basically, they start a friendly competition (usually friendly) to get your business. Lots of them will be appealing. That's because it's a buyers market - good news for you.

Each responder will provide some background information along with their offer. There will be navigable links you can click on to review their history with Elance, their portfolio, and ratings given by some of their clients. Unsubscribed web surfers will not have access to all the detail that you do on the ghostwriters. Likewise, casual surfers will not have access to all of your ad's details either. From the bids you get, you read up on the materials available and make a selection.

Once you've awarded the project to a writer, you'll work up an agreement between you and the writer, and arrange payment through Elance. There are agreement templates you can use on the site, and there are recommended methods of paying also. You may want to browse through some of this information early on regarding scheduling and payment, even before you place your ad, to make sure you understand the "fine print." There's nothing terrible there that I know of, but read it all anyway because it's the smart thing to do.

Payment can be made before the writing starts, after the writing is completed, or half before and half after the writing is completed. When you do pay, a percentage will be taken by Elance. This fee is currently less than

10 percent and is considered a finder's fee. Basically, you won't pay anything to your ghostwriter or to the databank service until you have actually selected a writer.

Guru operates similarly. You can visit www.guru.com to find the company's agreements, paying procedures, and finder's fee amounts. The home page of Guru lists categories of freelancers available. You will want to head directly to the "Writing/Editing/Translation" category list on Guru. Currently, there's a fee structure at Guru that varies depending on what type of subscription freelancers or service companies have purchased. Some freelancers can list basic skills and respond to some ads for free. Paid members and companies will have higher profiles and be able to bid more frequently. To post a "ghostwriter wanted" ad is free. You will still have the power to peruse the entire catalog and invite certain service providers to bid on your project. The finder's fees range from 5 to 10 percent, and the finder's fees are pulled from the buyer and/or the seller at Guru.

Guru is a larger site that has won some awards and has a catalog of hundreds of thousands of service providers in their database. Like with Elance, only a fraction of the service providers are ghostwriters looking for ebook work though. But a fraction of almost 500,000 is a good number.

Because of the buyers market, your odds are pretty good for finding someone quickly on the Internet. Postings for "ghostwriter wanted" are a factor of ten fewer than the number of authors that may bid on the job. This is regardless of monthly fees and percentages charged to the writers on the sites. Sometimes there's also a fee-per-bid charge for service providers. Since many ghostwriters who will be responding to your ad are already out of pocket monetarily, they're eager for your project. And, they are serious about their business.

The information available about each service provider, i.e. ghostwriter, can be compared to information available on vendors on the popular eBay auction site. Histories and rankings on the large sites are readily available for each writer or company you are thinking of hiring. You can see if other clients have been satisfied with a writer's work, and see how many ebooks a ghostwriter has written through the use of the freelancer bank. These indicators can be very helpful when it comes time to make a selection, and I'll talk more about how to choose a writer in the next chapter.

There is another freelance database on the web where ghostwriters lurk sometimes called AllFreelance. Luckily it's SHUT down now. There, ebook creators have been known to find ghostwriters using a procedure similar to the ones at Elance or Guru. Ads are placed, and freelance writers respond with bids. I don't like the site myself because of the irritating popups. But, it's got some traffic. I'm a busy man, focused on what I want to get done, and therefore I personally don't generally return to popup sites (as you may be able to tell by now!).

If you don't want the project details public

You may not wish to reveal your one-of-a-kind ebook subject or title to just anybody in what amounts to a classified ad. But you still want to attract competing ghostwriters to your interesting project. Here's what you can do. Both of the freelance database sites provide a mechanism for you to post some information in your ad that only the paid subscribers can see. This is a good way to go, and you'll see during your initial browse of others' ads that many advertisers do this. You'll see a symbol next to the project listing that indicates some of the detail is locked from public view. Already, portions of the ads are hidden from public view, and extra "locking" reduces the visible portions even further.

Also, you can be vague in your ad. There's no need to list your title, ideas of chapters, or even the precise nature of the subject matter. In your ad, you can call your project a "business ebook," if you like.

When you hire a ghostwriter, you will of course need to deliver the particulars so that they can do a great job for you. Even then, it's common to have the writer sign a confidentiality agreement. So, basically, don't worry too much about someone else seeing your idea before your ebook is done. The threat of a book idea or title being stolen is not really that high, although as mentioned earlier, ideas are not copyrighted, so someone could rightfully go running off with your idea. The truth is any reader of your book or related sales web site could swipe your ideas just as easily. Regardless of the risks, try not to deliberate or worry excessively. I'm sure you are busy too, and you have better things to do.

You may wonder why the ads are made visible to the public at all. The sites make all ads available in partial form so that unsubscribed visitors may, by viewing samples, be enticed to become members. Everyone starts as a browser and needs something to browse before making larger decisions.

As you browse, you will surely see that invariably, advertisers get some responses that are outrageous. Offers to write a 100 page book in a day for a few hundred bucks. At this stage, just ignore those, and know that regardless of a few sour grapes, overall the system tends to work.

You can move things along a little in terms of trying to get the type of responders you want. Obviously, offering a legitimate amount of time and pay is one way to attract a good ghostwriter. On Elance, you can peruse the database and select certain writers to invite them to bid on your project. On Guru, you can screen out certain types of people from the list to bid on your project.

Once you get to the list on Elance, follow the site's instructions to invite certain people to bid on your project. You can either browse through the list line by line, and select candidates you like to invite, or you can do a site search for certain types of qualifications. There's usually a limit on how many freelancers you can "invite" to bid. Ten or fifteen writers should be plenty though. The sites limit invitees to keep advertisers from mass-inviting the whole list. That would serve no purpose since ads are viewable by all members, but some advertisers would surely mass-invite to be more visible than competing projects. Limiting invitees takes care of that potential problem.

On Guru, you can limit your ad allowing only writers with certain qualifications to bid. Because Guru's database is so large, most advertisers screen out writers who do not have paid memberships. This, in theory, eliminates fly-by-night writers who are not willing to pay or to maintain a monthly subscription to the service.

On Elance and Guru, most ebooks are outsourced for a flat fee. When I say flat fee, I'm talking about the money you offer to pay the ghostwriter (as opposed to the various percentages and fees taken by the database site). If you choose to, you may, in addition to the flat fee, offer a ghostwriter a per-sale percentage. This is a good-hearted thing to do, since the writer created the work. Even ghostwriters have to live. You are never under any obligation, and most ebook owners don't offer percentages to their ghostwriters.

You will be required to use the payment processors on the sites, so that they can take the appropriate percentages, and also so that the writer is somewhat guaranteed to receive proper payment. For example, on Guru, some writers may opt only to receive payments through an escrow plan. By doing so, they require that their clients have the payment available in full in an escrow account. Although actually payment is not transferred until agreed terms are met, the money is sitting in the account, to be paid upon completion. Having the money sitting in escrow builds a writer's trust in your ability to pay.

You also may if you wish offer credit to your ghostwriter in your ebook. It's occasionally a common practice with paper books, and you may do the same in your ebook.

I recommend it, because it's a nice thing to do and will please a good writer who you want to remain on good terms with. Here's how you do it without flat-out telling readers your book was ghostwritten. 1) Thank them by name in an acknowledgments paragraph. Don't mention what exactly you're thanking them for. Your acknowledgments paragraph can be in a foreward, and introduction, or near the end of the ebook. 2) Include the ghostwriter name in the byline in an inconspicuous location in the beginning of your ebook. Don't do this on the cover or in your web sales ad, and don't make it prominent. In small print underneath "by" Your Name, include the phrase "with Gary Ghostwriter." 3) Instead of using "with," use "as told by."

I wouldn't go as far as to say that giving partial credit is a universal practice, especially with ebooks, but it is done, so you might want to think about it. I do it sometimes, but not all the time with ebook ghostwriters. I decide based on the quality of their work, the possibility of follow-on ebooks, and whether or not the readership would be compromised in any way.

Here's why I'm telling you the partial credit stuff: even though it's something you can offer that is often considered as good as compensation, I do not recommend that you offer it outright on the database sites. Regardless of what other advertisers are offering, only offer partial credit if the final product warrants it. I implement partial credit on a case by case basis, and never offer it to an unknown writer up front.

Alternative to Writer Banks

Frankly, placing your project ad into a large database like one on Elance or Guru and getting competing bids is the most efficient way to find a ghostwriter. However, I would be remiss if I didn't at least let you know that there are some ghostwriters that you can hire directly. I mentioned you could look around in writing organizations, but also, you can go directly to any of the web sites listed in the last section of this book. You will need to do your homework, check references, etc. on any of these ghostwriters, just as you would with ghostwriters on the database sites.

To find more individual ghostwriting web sites, search the Internet for "ghostwriting service," or "ebook ghostwriters."

If you hire directly, you will save yourself the finder's fee charged by the database web sites. However, you will not have access to the competitive marketplace and the ranking information from the large sites. On Elance and Guru, after projects are completed, many clients provide some very valuable and useful feedback on their experiences with the ghostwriters they hired. This feedback is available to future clients and people who are placing ads.

Individuals and companies who provide ghostwriting services but are not bidding for your job through Elance or Guru may charge flat fees, percentages, or per-page rates. Some require partial credit in the ebook. Some of them advertise rates that are rather high compared to the ghostwriter banks, but you may also find some that are comparable, try Google.

Talk to individual-site potential ghostwriters online to find out their fees, experience, and such. If one can't help you, he or she may be able to direct you to someone else in their line of work that can.

However you go about finding one of the many ghostwriters that are lurking day and night, for efficiency's sake, do use the Internet. Post your project on Guru or Elance or both, or initiate contact with an online ghostwriting service. Once you start getting bids from the banks and/or pricing and service information from the individual ghostwriting services, you'll have decisions to make, and I'll tell you how to choose a writer in the next chapter.

Some tips on posting your ghostwriter wanted ad

Back to the database sites, posting an ad is simple once you have your topic or title selected. You want to include some particulars, but not all of them at this stage. (Once you negotiate terms with a writer, then you will of course put every item that you require into a contract.)

Your ad should include the following items:

1. Short description of the project. A few lines at most.
2. Maximum amount you are willing to pay. Writers can bid lower than this, but they cannot bid above your maximum offering for your project.
3. Date you will close bidding on your project. Close bidding in a few days or a few weeks. Don't leave your ad lingering on the site too much longer than that, because it loses momentum. Besides, if you are not getting responses you like, you can always place another.
4. Deadline the ghostwriter will have to meet. Give the writer a month or six weeks if you can. But, if you really need a book in seven days or less, then specify that.

If, for example, you'd like to have a book written on the subject of how to homeschool your gifted child, here is some text you might include in your ad.

1. An 80-page or longer ebook covering successful homeschooling techniques to use specifically with gifted

children. Research to be done by the writer. Two revisions if necessary.

2. Maximum acceptable bid: $1200.
3. Close bidding date: 12/05/05.
4. Will need completed book within 21 days of job start.

Tip: *A good length for a for-sale ebook is 80 pages. Other common lengths are 40, 60, or 100 pages. To specify that you'd like an 80-page ebook, require at least 80 pages, or 80 pages + in your post. A free-give-away ebook used to market other products or services may be any length.*

You can specify any other parts of the book you like, but keep your list of requirements relatively short. For example, you may specify that you need a glossary chapter or that you will need drawings and/or photographs included. For a book on how to tie your own flies, you may ask that the ghostwriter provide drawings, or you may provide the drawings yourself. The former is easier for you, but will probably drive the cost and delivery time up somewhat.

When you come to an agreement with a writer, you will naturally provide all the other details he or she will need to complete the book. He may need to know what font you would like or what personal details you want included.

It is a good bargain to pay around $1,000 to get an 80-page ebook ghostwritten without drawings, photographs, or cover art included. It is possible to get good ghostwriters sometimes for a tad less. If you offer to pay a maximum of $150 for an 80-page book, you will not likely get a ghostwriter who knows what he is doing. You can advertise a maximum of $1,000 for a 60-page ebook, and you will get some legitimate offers in the range of $500 to $1,000. Although you don't want to pay a huge amount more than necessary, I do recommend that you offer and pay an adequate amount to get a good ghostwriter. It's worth it.

My rule is for a simple ebook, I will pay up to $1500. I add more if drawings or photographs are required or if length is greater than 80 pages. My math indicates that I will need to sell roughly 100 ebooks to recoup that money. No problem, since I'm working the marketing and sales end instead of writing the book. And my sales are much higher, generally.

Tell viewers what kind of qualifications you are looking for. Either make the selection on the screen by clicking on the categories provided by the service, or indicate clearly in the text of the ad what type of person you're looking for.

You will also want to indicate that you may require that the ghostwriter make revisions after you review the ebook. Note this in your ad as well. It is okay to indicate that you would like two sets of possible revisions to be included in the bid. When you negotiate the final terms with the writer, you can specify what types of revisions are included and the timeframes for them to be done.

One thing you do not want to do is to change your mind on what you want after you have already posted your ad. Although posting is free on the ad sites, if you make changes or otherwise renegotiate on terms already established, word will get out. Besides it's just not a good idea. It wastes your time.

A great way to make sure you've included all necessary details, but have not gone overboard with too much detail in the initial stages, is by browsing other ghostwriter-wanted ads Elance or Guru. In ten minutes, you'll be able to jot down your ad by using one of them as a template.

Posting projects (or, running your ad to find a ghostwriter) requires a little bit of reading time on your end. But once you learn how to post ads the first time, you can repeat the process over and over again with little effort whatsoever.

Do it your way with ghostwriters

Don't be fooled into thinking that you can have it your way with any other route. To get exactly what you want without writing it yourself, hire a competent ghostwriter. There is another way to sell or give away a book without having to write it. I'll tell you about it and then tell you why I don't much care for it.

Ebooks that have already been written are available for purchase. The process is often called "ebook reselling." You can actually buy, and pretty cheaply I might add - sometimes for less than a hundred bucks, a pre-written ebook. With the price, you obtain the license to resell. Then you can sell that ebook as many times as you like for any price you like.

A couple of Internet sites that do this are listed in the last chapter of this book in case you want to see how this is done for your own edification - but I actually do not recommend going this route.

I don't recommend ebook resales for several reasons. First, you don't get to create your own personal and unique book. Others will also have resale rights. The very customers you are trying to sell to may be also receiving marketing materials from someone else for the exact same book!

Second, many of these resale ebooks contain marketing information or links to other services which serve the purposes of the original writer and not you or your targeted readership. This is one of the ways that an originator gets by with selling the ebooks so cheaply for resale. He heads straight to the bank whenever a reader that you sold the book to buys one of his offered services or other ebooks.

Third, ebook resale services are heavy-handed with advertising. You can't even pay a visit to one of their web sites without getting bombarded with popups. Nobody likes over-the-top selling or advertising. In fact, no one likes sneaky, subtle advertising either. If your readers go back to the originating web site, which will most definitely be listed in the ebook, then they'll be bombarded too. With your own ghostwritten ebook, if you utilize advertising of your own services boldly or subtly, at least the advertising you're exposing to the readers is for products or services that you will receive compensation for. And then maybe you could resell **your** book...just something to think about.

Ghostwriting gives you a one-of-a-kind product. In the end, although someone else wrote it, you dreamed it up, and you own it outright. Ghostwritten ebooks, compared to resales, offer maximum flexibility for you to market, revise, advertise, and more. You can actually legally pursue anyone that tries to copy the written work or resell your ebook without your permission. You're protected by the copyright law. Pay the money to get a unique book created that you have control over. Pay extra to get an excellent ghostwriter if you need to (what I mean is don't always take the lowest bid necessarily). Then you will be proud to sell your well-written, distinctively-your-own, ebook.

Chapter 3

Finding Your Writer

Good news! After you place your first ad, within days if not minutes, you will likely have multiple freelancers who have responded wanting to ghostwrite your ebook. If you contacted any ghostwriting services outside the freelance banks, then you'll probably also get immediate responses and interest in your project. At that point, you will have the wonderful problem of having to choose which writer you'll use.

Why not just take the lowest bid?

You might be tempted to take the lowest bid, but if you are willing to invest only a few extra minutes, you could save yourself from heartache that might follow if all you are looking at is price. You need to find someone who will do a good job, deliver a timely result, and who is at least somewhat pleasant to work with.

First, read all details that each bidder has posted in response to your ad. Look for writers who have verified **credentials** and who have had positive client reviews at Elance or Guru. Verified credentials are those for which the site received confirmation in official form, such as a transcript or diploma.

Review **customer ratings** that have been posted on Elance or Guru. This type of feedback will not be available from individual ghostwriting sites, but is readily available on the database sites. Not all clients post feedback after a project because they get in a hurry or forget. But many do. And you can usually put some stake in the ratings because the clients were once in your shoes placing an ad for a similar service in the databank. Therefore the databank clients' feedback ratings and comments are not irrelevant. Clients' comments help you see if they were satisfied with the working relationship and also with the quality of the finished product.

For ghostwriting services obtained through Elance, Guru, or an individual ghostwriter site, check out the writer's **references**. Don't just look at a list of names and assume that the longer the list, the better the references. Get contact information, and follow up. Contact the references; that's what they're there for. Reference lists and testimonials are only as good as the phone numbers that come with them so that you can confirm that someone was satisfied with the work.

It is the nature of ghostwriting that the ghostwriter is not at liberty to divulge or show you his work for others. But if you could speak to only one of his or her clients or collaborators, then at least that is something. Be hesitant to award your first project to a writer who will not provide at least one reference of some kind!

Where ratings and references will tell you how easy or difficult a writer may be to work with, **writing samples** will give you a more explicit idea of how well a writer actually writes. Although ghostwriters are not at liberty to post or publish work they did for others for a flat fee, they may be able to show you something they wrote for their own benefit or something that they published under their own name. In occasional cases, ghostwriters are given credit in the books (or ebooks) that they wrote. Those books would be good writing samples to look at. Require at least one or two writing samples at a minimum. An experienced ghostwriter should have a lengthy portfolio, but even a lesser experienced ghostwriter should be able to show you something they've written. Even a letter to the editor of a newspaper or an essay on their personal web site is better than nothing. You can tell a lot about writers from their samples. You can usually tell if they speak conversationally, if they have a comfortable command of the language you're looking for, and if they pay attention to detail (with no errors spelling or punctuation).

In addition to ratings, references and writing samples, you may want to also ask that your ghostwriter be fluent or proficient in a particular **language**. You may even request a native speaker if you like. Do ask, because when you are evaluating bulleted online information like job bids, you cannot always tell who speaks what language fluently. Short bids with line items that are purely factual are easily done by native or non-native speakers. The nature of the online bidding is that short and sweet is better than long and beautifully written. So don't base much on the bid. Read the ratings, contact a reference, review a writing sample, and request a native speaker. He who speaks a language well and fluently is more likely to write it well and fluently. That's what you want for your ebook.

Although terse ad responses are common, if you do see any glaring errors in the response to your ad, like a misspelled word or confusing explanations, proceed with caution in the direction of that writer. Give a responder some leeway in abbreviating or being direct. Beyond that, glaring errors in can be an indicator that the responder may not be the best one for your project. Remember, if you wanted to slap a book together throwing grammatical caution to the wind, you could write that yourself. You are looking for a skilled writer who pays attention to details.

Again, beware of responders offering to write you a 100-page ebook in a matter of days. If you want any kind of in-depth coverage or research, this isn't possible, even for a talented and experienced ghostwriter. These people are trying to steal your business away from bona fide writing professionals. Skim past outrageous ads; don't waste your time there.

It's not to say that an amateur wouldn't do a good job, it's just that with experience comes better writing that is faster and more accurate. Even the best ghostwriter cannot perform miracles. He or she will need time to read, study, interview, organize, draft, and revise before getting it to you.

Regarding amateurs, if you think that someone with little or no ebook writing experience would be a good fit for your ebook anyway, then you may be right. Everyone, even a ghostwriter, has to start somewhere. Although he may not have many client ratings on the site, he should be able to get you a resume, some writing samples, and some general business references. If a new ghostwriter is serious, he will have prepared these items. You don't go to a job interview without a resume in hand, do you? Well ghostwriters that are ambitious and have talent, likewise will be able to show it. Review the resume and writing samples, and contact the references, Then, who knows, you may find that you and he are a great fit. You may strike gold where other potential clients have walked on by.

As I mentioned, be extremely wary of **outrageous claims**. If a writer can't provide you with any verification that he has indeed written over 200 ebooks and made his clients over ten million dollars, then there is no reason to believe it. Nor is it generally possible to get any kind of quality book written in a matter of days. If you get tempted to use one of these mavericks, check their feedback from other clients. You may get the real picture there. If it seems too good to be possibly true, it is. Use common sense.

More on client rankings

On Elance and Guru, when you open your ad, you will see a list of the bidders who responded, how much they propose to charge, and some links to check out their qualifications. One of the links will take you to a **responder's profile page**. Go there and read all the entries carefully. You can glean what others in the system think about the writer's work - both the work product and how easy he or she was to work with.

As you're reviewing, keep in mind that just as some responders can be outrageous, so can some advertisers. It is possible that Client A advertised that he wanted a particular ebook written. Writer B responded; they worked out mutually acceptable terms. Writer B, an experienced ghostwriter, went straight to work, and produced a product that was exactly as required by the ad, the agreement, and his general good judgment and experience. Yet, Client A was not satisfied. Client A decided mid- project that he wished he would have remembered his niece was a writer, and he thinks he should have hired someone in the family. Writer B knows nothing of this and continues to write per the agreement. Client A becomes grudging and difficult during the writing process. He is never quite satisfied with the ebook, although Writer B doesn't ever understand completely why.

Eventually the ebook project is completed and payment is delivered, but Client A, still unhappy in his world, gives Writer B a low ranking and zero kudos even though Writer B did a fine job.

This kind of stuff happens; so what you want to do is look at multiple rankings. One or two outliers can pretty well be ignored. In any case, a single low mark or a single high mark probably doesn't mean as much as overall in terms of how clients are appraising this person's work. Look for how **most** clients ranked this person. Also compare that against how many jobs the responder has actually done. Fifty fairly positive ratings would be a safer bet than a single stellar rating.

Before you seal the deal

Once you go through the items above, you will have a good feel about who to select from the list for your project. You may have six really good contenders. In that case, take the one with the best writing samples.

The benefits of searching the databanks are many. However, one drawback is that you cannot always make direct contact with prospective ghostwriters. Sometimes you can. But on individual ghostwriter sites, you will usually be able to get in touch with and talk to the actual ghostwriter. This is one more way to make sure that you feel 100 percent comfortable with your decision.

So, where possible, contact the ghostwriter directly. Get to know him a little. Lots of things cannot be translated over the Internet, but you can figure out a lot in a quick phone call. You may **ask questions** such as, "Will you be writing yourself, or will you be giving this job to one of your employees?" You have the right to find out such things.

One key that a ghostwriter is good is **repeat business**. Repeat business indicates that a client liked the ghostwriter's work because the client came back for more. On the database sites, you can see from the profile page if a client has posted more than one rating for more than one project on that particular ghostwriter. If there are multiple project entries from the same client, smile, and move that ghostwriter to the top of your list.

I don't think this is as big of a deal, but it is something to look for: **areas of expertise**. If your book is on running a house on a tighter budget, and a ghostwriter with good credentials, references, samples, ratings, and some repeat business also has experience writing books about money - bingo. It just doesn't get any better than that.

I've warned against believing outrageous claims to write your book for next to nothing in less time than it takes to get a suit dry cleaned. Now I'd like to mention the writers on the other end of the spectrum. There are some writers who just plain **charge beyond the top end** for their services. Some are out to take your money, hoping you'll stumble on their web site, and be dumb enough not to check out the going rate to get a book published on a databank site, and you'll pay their fee schedule, no matter that it's above industry standard.

Now, some men and women who charge an arm and a leg are actually extremely gifted and highly-sought-after artists. You may be tempted to get one of them because they've done writing for a famous client list or they've been published in the New York Times.

But don't. Don't hire the over-charger, and don't hire the Rolls Royce of ghostwriters. Neither one will get you what you need. With the over-charger, you'll be paying too much for a product. With the Rolls Royce writer, you will get better writing than you need for a book. Your target readers, in most cases, are hungry for information. They want a book that cuts through the bull, lays the dots out, and then connects them. They don't want a lot of three or four syllable words. They don't require or appreciate poetry or line after line of clever humor. There's just no need to have J. K. Rowlings write your book (and anonymously, imagine!).

If for some reason after reading this book, you decide not to use a ghostwriter bank system to get competing bids, then I urge you to **comparison shop**. Get at least three bids if you're looking only at individual ghostwriting sites.

Generally, if a ghostwriter wants $10,000 for a 60-page ebook, he's charging more than normal. I can't think of anything that would make this worth the money. If she claims to be able to complete your project in 48 hours or less, in my experience, the product will be sloppy at best.

If a ghostwriter wants $5,000 for an 80-page ebook, she's charging on the high side, but you may want to see if the services are worth it. She may score an A-plus on every criterion mentioned in this chapter, and she may indeed be your niece! In that case, I wouldn't think of stopping you. Some writers offer a range of additional services, guarantees, rewrites, or even prepare cover art or sales web pages for you. Ghostwriters are an eclectic bunch. Some may even provide you with marketing leads. Still, I think $5,000 is on the high side, and I'd try to look for someone a couple thousand dollars cheaper, just because I can in the buyers market. (But don't tell my brother's daughter.)

When you select a writer, you will need to strike up a **written agreement**. The large freelancing sites have contracts that you can use. The contracts will include payment for particular milestones, whether or not revisions will be included, deadlines, and confidentiality issues. Use the standard contracts as starting points. You may want to have an attorney check out the legalese, but from my experience the templates are good. Use them. From individual ghostwriting sites, you certainly want to carefully read, negotiate, and possibly have an attorney review your contracts and work agreements.

Prepare for future projects

What makes a great ghostwriter? Here's what: a reasonable price, timely delivery, a good product, and something else. Yes, something else! The icing on the cake is a good, trust-based, long-term working relationship. If you **develop a relationship** with a good ghostwriter, you can bring him or her project after project, and accomplish all kinds of goals with his or her help. A good ghostwriter at your disposal is as good as gold.

So lay the groundwork for finding and keeping a good ghostwriter associate. Pay reasonable rates. Don't belittle your writer, and don't expect them to stay awake at night without food or sleep to complete your projects. The ghostwriter is a freelancer, not your employee. As such, he is at liberty to work in the best way possible at his own discretion. If your ghostwriter is particularly good, tell others who might hire him. Bringing in business will always earn you high marks. Pay promptly when jobs are finished. Never withhold payment if the terms of the agreement have been met. Give your favorite ghostwriter interesting new subjects to write about. Tell him he did a good job! Give him partial credit if it will not adversely affect your ebook. Go back to the previous chapter of this ebook to review ways you can slip his or her name in without giving up the secret that your ebook was ghostwritten.

Obviously I have a lot of respect for ghostwriters. Even though I'm not willing to pay what Britney Spears would for an autobiography, I am willing to pay on high end of the ebook pay scale. I like to write, don't get me wrong, it's just that ghostwriters can really write. They know things that I don't even want to know and see details that I don't want to be bothered with. In my experience, it's easy to find a ghostwriter and not quite as easy to find a really good one.

Once I've found a good one or two, I do my best to keep them happy and keep them around. This saves me time, money, and frustration. Once you develop a small group of good ghostwriters for yourself, there's almost no end to the number of ebooks you can write in a year.

Think long-term when you work with a ghostwriter. You can interview new ghostwriters for every project, which isn't difficult, just time-consuming. Or, you can develop a relationship with one or more excellent ghostwriters and save yourself from all that trouble. Treat your good ghostwriter with respect and courtesy, and your investment will come back to you many-fold!

How to find a book cover art designer

Just like searching for a ghostwriter, you could ask and call around in your community's art organizations to find artists that you could pay to design a book cover for you.

Another way to do it is to conduct an Internet search. If you type in key words "ebook cover art" you'll get pages and pages of results. Ebook cover artists are literally standing by to get your project on the world wide web. Some individuals specialize in ebook cover art, and some companies provide a gamut of graphics or e-selling services.

The reality is, going to individual web sites and researching each one can take some time. So, I would invite you to try one of my low-B.S. approaches to finding a book cover art designer.

Here's what you do: Look at web sites where ebooks are being sold. Most well-marketed ebooks have cover art shown on a web page where the ebook(s) can be purchased. Decide for yourself which of the ebook covers most capture your attention and would therefore be good for your project.

Once you've found one or two really great ebook covers, contact the webmasters and ask who did the designs. You'd be surprised how many people will share their information with you. Introduce yourself pleasantly. You won't find out much by being gruff or unfriendly. Be honest and open, and if you want to start off on the right foot, it may help you get in the door if you initiate the conversation by complimenting the webmaster's work. When you're using your best manners, if one webmaster won't divulge his cover art designer, then another webmaster definitely will.

How to choose a designer

A good designer works with you and for you.

Whether by Google or by referral, once you navigate to a book cover designer's web page, read through her terms to see what her fee is, how well she works with people, and any examples of her work. Contact her to get additional information. And regardless of any testimonials on her web page, ask for references of real people whom you can contact yourself.

Look for things like:

- Does the artist get a lot of repeat business?
- Has the artist been responsive to your questions?
- Have you seen some excellent examples that you really like?
- Does the artist guarantee your satisfaction before he gets full payment?
- Will turnaround be a few days? (It really shouldn't take more than a week at any rate.)
- Will he or she revise the artwork after you've seen the first draft? Is this revision included in the quoted cost?
- Do you feel yourself wanting to buy the ebooks shown on the designer's web page that this designer "covered"? In other words, do his or her pictures entice you to make an immediate purchase?
- Will the artist also be able to create additional items like web page headers, banners, or related items?

The work to weed out designers and to find a few that you like will pay for itself in the long run when you want to create ebook after ebook. It's good to have someone who designs great covers, whom you can trust and rely on, who works quickly and effectively, and who charges reasonable rates.

> *Tip:* *Find out the web services fees when you're asking about ebook cover art fees. It's an added perk if your ebook cover artist also provides web page design services. You may wish to have your marketing web page and ebook cover design match. A good artist can generate titles, banners, buttons, and other related web page items.*

What Makes a Great Book Cover?

When you hire a designer, you're giving up the reins on your cover art to some extent. You can definitely use your gut instinct (which is usually right anyway) to determine when a cover is just right for your ebook. If your gut doesn't speak to you, you can also make sure your cover art is good by asking yourself and answering some questions.

Does the artwork stand out proudly on your web page? You don't want it to blend in with the background or be barely noticeable. Whether it's by color, texture, shape, exclamation points, or professional looking artwork, your designer needs to know how to add enough pizzazz to your cover art to get you noticed. This doesn't mean that you need microscopic detail or complicated figures or drawings. Sometimes simplicity does the job quite well. Artists know that. Look for the "stand out" factor on his designs.

Is the title prominent on the cover? You don't want too many words on the cover. Stick with the title, a byline, and short words. You may be able to effectively include a short bulleted list, but not much more. When you quickly scroll through web pages, you should be able to remember from a quick glance what the title was on your ebook cover. If the title isn't lodged in your memory after a passing glance at the picture, then the artwork needs a face lift.

Does the cover use four colors or less? Although rainbows are pretty, they don't stand out as much as solid colors. You can actually get by with three colors. In most cases, you'll need at least one more color besides just black and white. Just like web pages can look unprofessional with too many animated graphics and background textures (moon craters, wood grain, tiles with photographs on them, whatever), likewise, your cover does not require all these frills. Don't be sold on an artist or his work because he can make your ebook cover look like a tie-dyed T-shirt. Unless of course your book is about tie-dying! Occasionally lots of colors or textures are called for, but usually not.

Can you read each letter of text on the cover? You do not want a font that is difficult to discern. Interestingly, the simple fonts that we use every day when we communicate by email, are some of the best for ebook cover art. There's a reason fonts like Arial and Times are so popular. People find them easy to read. Don't make your potential buyers work to hard to figure out which letter is which on your cover. In general, stay away from curly cues, unusual handwriting fonts, and heavily detailed lettering.

Does your cover have a large amount of red, blue, or yellow? These have been determined by psychologists to be appealing colors for consumers. In fact any two of these colors in combination with black and white would probably work. Steer away from brown, green, gray, and muted or faded colors unless there is some really good reason to use those colors. For example if your book is called "How to build a log cabin," your project may be well-served by browns and greens. But maybe not! Try red, blue, yellow, black and white first to see! By the same token, money ebooks do not have to be green, and ebooks for brides do not have to be white.

Does your cover look like a three-dimensional object? You are trying to convey an actual book, so you definitely want the art in 3-D. Make sure your ebook art has a spine and the appearance of some internal pages. Don't settle for a rectangular representation of only the front cover of a book. A flat rectangle could work for the first page inside your book, but not for a picture on a web site that is supposed to attract a buyer. Even though your readers will obviously have enough computer wherewithal to have found your ebook in the first place, in their hearts, they will still be attracted to online artwork that reminds them of actual paper books. It's just a fact of life, so accept it, and make sure your ebook cover art looks like a book.

Researching Your Book

This is the part of this book that makes it worth all you paid for it and about a thousand dollars more - web resources and links that I've compiled in all of my research and experience.

For the most part, the items listed in this chapter have been discussed or mentioned in previous chapters. In some cases, I've listed web sites here just for your information, so you can see how a site is laid out or see just how many vendors are available. Where a site is recommended, I'll say so.

Whether I recommend a site or not, I would like to let you know that I am in no way affiliated with these companies or individuals. I will not be making money if you visit these sites, and they have not paid for advertising in this ebook. (This ebook is for you, and there are no strings attached.) Therefore, as you bounce around the Internet, check references where necessary, and feel free to use other services that you may have discovered along the way.

Ebook ghostwriters

www.elance.com - As discussed at length in Chapter 1, this site has a large bank, or database, of ghostwriters looking for work. You can place an ad here and wait for offers to come in.

www.guru.com - Like Elance only bigger by almost a factor of ten, Guru also has a database of ghostwriters looking for work.

Recap

Whew! I hope you've enjoyed learning about how to get your own book written even if you don't write yourself. When you outsource your book, you will be investing a little money, but saving a bundle in time, and you can get all your investment back and more. And just think - your hardest task was coming up with what your book would be about! The rest can be outsourced or done in rapid fashion by following the advice and tips in this book.

I'm glad you are interested in getting on the book bandwagon! I've enjoyed my experience with creating and selling books on the Internet, although I have to admit I stumbled and made some glorious mistakes early on in my learning curve. Your journey will be smoother than mine. However, if you encounter a few bumps on the road, dust off and get back in the game.